The Ultim
CATS' CATALOG

by
Ray G. Strobel

Photo Manipulation by
Parchment & Palette
Wisconsin Dells, WI

Produced by
Strobooks LLC

Andrews McMeel
Publishing
Kansas City

Dedicated to my lovely wife, Jo Belle, and
in memory of our wonderful one-eyed cat, Bruce,
who met an untimely death last year.

04   05   06   07   08   WKT   10   9   8   7   6   5   4   3   2   1

ISBN: 0-7407-4207-8

Library of Congress Control Number: 2003113276

A Note from Our Founder

Bruce the one-eyed cat

Dear Feline Friend—

I share your suffering. In this human-centric world it's virtually impossible to find high-quality products created with feline needs and requirements in mind.

I spent a lifetime (or so it seems) receiving stupid toys from my well-meaning humans. But one more catnip ball I could not take!

Where is the intellectual stimulation, I asked? Where are those gifts that feed our boundless ego? The beauty aids to address our narcissism?

That's why I founded **The Ultimate Cats' Catalog Company.** Just for you and all of your feline friends.

On the following pages you will find the products and gifts you've been looking for. And I will continue to search out and uncover those special items that make being a cat even better than it already is.

You can rest assured, "Eye's on it!"

Bruce

Watch for this graphic element

To keep our prices low, we regularly accept paid advertising in our catalog. However, we have checked out all these products and can recommend them highly. Just because they pay us big bucks for their ads is no reason to believe that we would steer you wrong. Trust us.

Our friendly staff says:
Welcome to the Ultimate Cats' Catalog!

We'll do our best to serve you in any way we can. If you don't see exactly what you want, just give us a call and we'll try to include it in our next catalog.

—Fluffy, Snuggles, and Max

Our Exclusive "Cat's Meow"
100% Guarantee

If you're not forced to exclaim *"Now ain't that the cat's meow!"* when you receive any item from our catalog, we will promptly refund your money, no questions asked.

Snuggles
Senior Customer Service Cat

Gift certificates available. Just ask!

Feline Tummy Tucker

Lost that girlish figure after the 3rd litter?

Kick that spare tire in your spare time

You're not alone. After 3 or 4 litters we all start to sag a bit. And those extra calories from excessive treats over the years don't help either. So—what to do about that unsightly bulge around your middle?

Of course, exercise is out of the question. Aside from being so unfeline, it tends to interfere with valuable nap time.

Your perfect solution is our exclusive Feline Tummy Tucker. It works while you nap so you get the gain without the pain (just like humans).

Just strap it on (paw-friendly Velcro® pads make it easy), and you'll be back in fightin' form in just days. Trust us.

(Arrives in plain brown wrapper.)

Before   After

Adjustable Velcro® straps!

AS SEEN ON TV

Item #4445
Feline Tummy Tucker..............$14.95

Change/Don't Change Litter Flag

Just like the fancy hotels

"Hey, can't you see I'm busy?!"

One just can't seem to get decent service anymore! Either you're in the middle of a quiet "moment" when some insensitive human barges in and wants to change the litter, or they don't show up for days and you're faced with a minefield when you want to do your business.

We looked to major four-star hotels to help us solve this problem and their expertise helped us develop the perfect solution. One side of the durable, acrylic flag politely requests *"Do Not Disturb,"* while the other demands, *"Hey, can't you smell anything? Change it!"*

Just a flip of the paw aims the flag in the proper direction and finally you get the service you deserve. Instantly clips to any standard-size litter box. Available in English, Spanish, French, Urdu, or German.

DO NOT DISTURB!

HEY! CHANGE IT!

Item #2243
Litter Change Flag (mounting hardware included)..........$7.95

Easy Rider Cat Carrier

You've got the attitude, now here's your chance
Go "Hog" wild!

We must confess to our love affair with the classic movie *Easy Rider*. As Fonda and Hopper go roaring down the freeway our paws start a-tappin' as we dream of joining them on the open road.

Leave those boring pickups to the doggies; you've got the attitude it takes to ride the *big bikes* and now here's your chance! Our feline lounge-style carrier is heavy-duty chrome (of course) with black leather inserts for that "Don't mess with me" look.

As they always say on TV: *And that's not all!* Simply lift the seat to discover a built-in litter box that makes pit stops necessary only when you get a craving for a longneck.

Don your goggles (see page 8) and your bandanna and let the fur fly!

Size: 12" x 16" x 8". Attaches easily to any bike 1,000 cc or more.

Please Observe Helmet Laws!

Shown: Peaches with her fashionable straw feline helmet.

Item #0091 Easy Rider Cat Carrier.............$74.95

Electronic Human Tracking System

Tired of getting caught?
Now be ready whenever they return!

Why, you ask in all sincerity, would I want to keep track of my human?

The answer is simple. You need to know when they're coming home so you can stop doing evil things and instead be waiting innocently when they arrive.

How many times have you been caught in the act—clawing the curtains or couch or digging into those leftovers that were thoughtfully left out on the counter? No more. Now you can have ample warning and plenty of time to cover your tracks (or to set things up so the dog gets blamed).

Range: 42.5 miles.

Requires 2 AAA batteries (not included).

Item #7706
Humi-Track System.................$19.95

Mousie Roll-Ups

An elegant holiday treat
Mice in every slice!

Sumptuous and hearty, these roll-ups are the choice of gourmet cats world-wide. Prepared from a centuries-old recipe, first mice are selected for their plumpness, then carefully wrapped with multiple layers of fresh spinach, pungent imported cheeses and fragrant spices.

Twenty-five hours of smoking followed by slow roasting adds the distinctive flavor that has made this dish an all-time favorite.

Slice paper thin and you'll be delighted by the silhouette of a little critter in every bite.

Microwavable. Keeps 6 years, opened or unopened.

Gift Wrapping Available

Item #9901
Mousie Roll-Ups, serves 4...............$11.95

Endless Curtain

Over 500' of fabric on each roll

Claw, claw, claw—the fun never runs out!

Over 500' of fabric on roll.

We all know how frustrating it can be when you've finally clawed the missus's best curtains to shreds and there's no more fun to be had. You sit and look forlornly at that meager pile of fabric, knowing you still have the energy to do much more damage.

Well cheer up! There's no need to curb your destructive tendencies. With the **Endless Curtain**, your clawing action gently tugs on the hidden mechanism and *voilà!* it keeps feeding fabric until you've had your fill!

Special feature: Humans have such poor taste when it comes to choosing the best textures for decorating. They never take our clawing requirements into consideration. Now you can select your own texture from the swatches below.

Select the fabric of your choice!

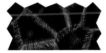 Wool
 Lace
 Burlap
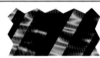 Silk

Item #4422 Endless Curtain..............$44.95
Refills (500')....................................$22.95

Urban Cat's Roadkill Press

Squash your own

Real highway taste <u>and texture</u>!

We get lots of mail from envious urban cats complaining about the lack of authentic road-kill treats in the big city.

And we agree. Why should only the country cats enjoy the pawing, the prying, and that ever-so-tasty aged meat of true road kill?

Here's the next best thing. A few turns of the screw and even the most high-rise of mice takes on that 18-wheel form and texture. No urban cat kitchen is complete without one. Now you can enjoy that country road-kill experience even in a studio apartment!

Made of 100% hardwood. Lasts a lifetime!

Item #9008
Roadkill Press......................................$24.95
Essence of asphalt flavoring, 8 oz. $2.95

Flyin' Feline® KneeSnoPad Snowboard

Velcro® yourself in
Wow! What a ride!

Fellow feline Felix from Finland faxed us to explain how he uses his human's kneepad to "surf the snow." His complaint was the pads didn't stand up to the rigorous demands of a snow loving cat like himself.

So we put our product development lab to work and they converted a nationally known heavy-duty kneepad to feline use with the addition of strategically placed cat-friendly Velcro® straps.

Now it's easy to head out to the backyard, strap yourself in, wax the bottom (see optional wax) and go for it! Ski wax and goggles sold separately.

Ask for pricing on our *Feline Fracture* insurance policies.

SOLD ONLY AS A SET OF TWO. GIVE ONE TO A FRIEND!

Item #1113
KneeSnoPad Snowboard (set of two) $12.95
Snow Goggles $8.95
Pad wax (optional)....................................$4.95

Pooch Pee Pouches

Spreads quickly and easily
Blame it on the pooch!

Did that bad dog make a mess <u>again</u>?

For those unfortunate felines who must share their domicile with a dog, here's the perfect way to put them in the doghouse (literally and figuratively).

Our unique **Pooch Pee Pouches** spread the smell of dog pee anywhere you place them . . . and guess who gets yelled at? After a few episodes we guarantee your canine nemesis will be banned to the doghouse and out of your hair.

Easy to use: Just place a pouch in an obvious spot and puncture the outer shell with your claw—it will dissolve instantly, leaving no trace while the pee oozes onto the surface making a smelly (and difficult to remove) spot.

Order a set of 12, enough to get a whole pack in trouble!

Item #9913
Pooch Pee Pouches (4).........................$6.95
Pooch Pee Pouches (12).....................$16.95

Viagria*—Cat Formula
Lost that frisky feeling?
Feel like an alley cat again or your money back!

Remember the good old days? You and the little lady could pump out a litter at the drop of a hat. And even if you were neutered, you still had the energy to run the streets and alleys for hours on end.

We know how it is—lately you've been feeling run-down, listless, lacking in that famous feline sex drive. Life has been reduced to just hanging around with your human cuddled up in front of a fire. Bo-oo-ring!

But wait, there's no need to count yourself out of the game just yet! Simply pop a pill for a powerful boost in sexual energy. That gleam will return to your eye and you'll feel like that good old alley cat again. Honest.

Caution: May cause minor side effects including fur loss, anxiety, loss of bladder control, halitosis, and excessive gas buildup.

Gift Wrapping Available

* Not to be confused with Viagra® or they might get mad at us. You know how big corporations never have a sense of humor.

"Worth every penny. Wow! It really works!"

"I must admit, I was a skeptic—but now I get some lovin' almost every night!"

—Fluffy, Lake Geneva, WI

Item #742 Viagria/Cats
3-month supply.............................$29.95
Large economy size.....................$45.95
"Till you drop" supply....................$95.95

Fur-to-Dye-4
Tired of looking like a common house cat?
The right color—the right look—for every occasion

Come on . . . go for it! It's time for a new look and you know it! Our amazing feline-friendly fur dyes can give you the look you've always dreamed about.

One application instantly converts calicos to sultry black cats, and boring gray to pure white (trust us).

A roll in your clean litter removes every last trace (no water required) so you can "dress up" for an evening on the prowl and be back to your old self in minutes.

Before	After	Before	After

"I'm normally kind of a dingy gray so I love the chance to dress up once in a while and be an orange tabby for a change of pace."

—Sally, Boston, MA

"On weekends, wow! . . your Fur-to-Dye-4 turns me into a Harley-driving, Camel-smoking black cat. The babes love it!"

—Brewster, Boston, MA

Item #6663
Fur-to-Dye-4 (12 oz. bottle)..........$12.95

Human Halloween Costume
Tired of being a black cat?
Be a human this year—it's real scary!

Last Year

This Year

Tired of being that cliché, a black cat, every year for Halloween and seeing your "take" diminish because of your lack of creativity? This is the year to be really frightening: Dress up like a human!

Just think, you'll be able to act real stupid and nobody will notice! Select from 3 classic human looks: Nordic American, African American, or Asian American. Whiskers tuck neatly behind realistic rubber face. Tail outlet provided.

Fire resistant. One size fits all.

Item #8920
Human Halloween Costume..............$11.95

The Croque Mouse-eur Maker
Take the tedium out of making this French delicacy
Ooh-la-la. Enjoy your meeses in the gourmet French style

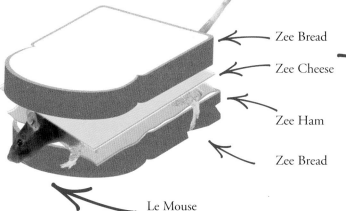

Zee Bread

Zee Cheese

Zee Ham

Zee Bread

Le Mouse

Les Frogs—zay know how to cook! They're famous for their Croque Monsieurs (toasted ham and cheese) and their Croque Madames (toasted ham, cheese, and egg). And now, directly from our test kitchen, comes this handy device to enable you to quickly and easily create their little-known delicacy: Le Croque Mouse-eur.

One-paw operation and the simple automatic 30-second timer makes fast food the French way. No messy clean up—dishwasher safe!

Item #4522 Croque Mouse-eur Maker..........$34.95

Fin of the Month Club
Created by chefs with cats!
Delicacies direct to your door

Ready to pop in the microwave to reheat, these complete gourmet dinners are no more than you deserve. Each month you receive a mouth-watering creation from America's most famous *cat loving chefs* (for obvious reasons chefs who keep dogs as pets were not invited to participate in this program). These selected chefs guarantee your meals are created just the way you've always dreamed (heavy on the anchovy reductions, catnip garnish, cream sauces, etc.)

January.	Salmon
February.	Trout
March.	Tuna
April	Bass
May	Goldfish
June.	Catfish
July.	Bluegill
August	Guppies
September	Perch
October	Swordfish
November.	Talapia
December.	Caviar!

CATS ONLY

Shipped in a plain brown wrapper so you can get to it first (you don't want your humans discovering you're dining better than they are).

Item #4422 Fin of the Month Club (12 shipments)..........$84.95

Organ Donation Program
Make a difference
Live on in Martina's racquet!

When your time comes (as it must) there's no need to just pass away. Now you—or at least your body parts—can live on and make someone else's life happier.

It's a shame to let a body like yours go to waste. Even when you're on your last legs your cat guts are a valuable asset. Here's all you need to do:

Ask for your Donor Application Card now (shown at right). Select either Guitar or Tennis Racquet and you're on your way to fame (but unfortunately, not fortune). As an added incentive you'll receive a beautiful "Thanks for your donation" treat assortment to enjoy while you're still alive and licking!

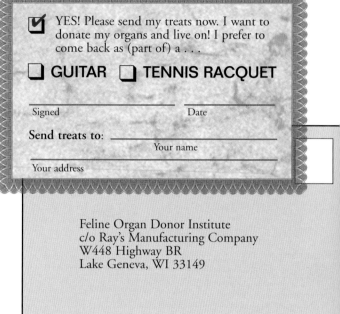

☑ **YES!** Please send my treats now. I want to donate my organs and live on! I prefer to come back as (part of) a . . .

❏ **GUITAR** ❏ **TENNIS RACQUET**

Signed _____ Date _____

Send treats to: _____
Your name

Your address _____

Feline Organ Donor Institute
c/o Ray's Manufacturing Company
W448 Highway BR
Lake Geneva, WI 33149

Item #2066
Organ Donor Card..........................No charge

24k Gold Tail Rings
Accessorize that tail
You've got it—flaunt it!

Come on now, admit it. Is there anything more beautiful than the feline tail? Humans seem to feel the need to draw attention to their rather ugly toes (and they say we're hard to understand) but a feline tail—that's another story!

These 24-karat gold tail rings were designed for us by one of Bulgaria's most famous jewelry designers. Flashy? Yes! But when you gently sway your tail as you shashay down the avenue, you'll thank us for adding a little more pizzazz to your life.

Lightweight so your tail stays up and in their face. We guarantee the boys will love them!

Select from the Cleopatra, the Brilliance, or the Classic. One size fits most tails.

Gift Wrapping Available

The Cleopatra

The Brilliance

The Classic

Item #9008 Tail Ring (please select style)............$24.95

NostalgiaCat® Calendar
Kool cats from the '30s, '40s, and '50s
When cats were cats!

Bring back the days of yesteryear (before Kitty Litter®) when having a cat as a companion required lots of patience—*and cats were really cats!* Featuring all the legendary cats from history, from Lucy's madcap feline, *Ba-Ba-Loo,* to that wild and crazy *Mr. President.* It seems felines lived faster and wilder in those days, just like their human companions. If your life is on the boring side, this is just the item to give you the inspiration to *move it up a notch!*

Famous Cat: *Flapper* Companion: *Zelda Fitzgerald*

Month	Famous Cat	Companion	Breed
Jan.	Mr. President	Marilyn Monroe	Alley Cat
Feb.	Isosceles	Albert Einstein	German Rex
Mar.	Ba-Ba-Loo	Lucy Arnez	Havana Brown
April	006	Ian Fleming	Classified
May	Rasputin	Anastasia	Russian Blue
June	Smokey	Dean Martin	American Bobtail
July	Pussy Dearest	Joan Crawford	Doll Face Persian
Aug.	Kojack	Yul Brenner	Hairless Siamese
Sept.	Pistol	Mae West	Chartreux
Oct.	John	Ayn Rand	Purebred
Nov.	Panorama	Ansel Adams	Tuxedo
Dec.	Flapper	Zelda Fitzgerald	Pixiebob

Item #9008 Calendar $24.95

Beautiful Kitten Claw Polish
Keep the boys howling—
Great shades for night and day

Oh, how you long for that grown-up look. You just can't wait to go out howling with the big girls but, face it, you're still just a kitten.

Well, there's nothing wrong with playing dress up with a little claw color to make you feel like a big girl.

Easy lick-off formula means you can get back to innocent-kitten mode when humans appear. Select from Feline Fuscia, Neon Green, or Real Red.

Item #0920 Claw Polish, each..................$11.95

Fiber-Optic "Nap Time" Doormat
Turns on/off automatically
Protects your valuable nap time

It's a fact of life: Guests always arrive when we're in the middle of our nap. When we're up we love company, but you know how we love our quiet time even more.

Now you can take control of your nap time with this space-age door mat. Millions of electronically controlled electronic fibers spell out *"Go Away . . . I'm Napping!"* when the timer clicks on and *"Welcome! I Hope You Brought Treats!"* when it turns off.

Factory preset timer is set for typical 20-hour-a-day cat nap time (you may reset timer if you prefer to sleep longer).

Item #5118
Fiber-Optic Door Mat $42.95

Designer Litter Box Liners
Interior design for your special place
Eat your heart out, Martha!

It's a good thing!

We spend a lot of time in our litter boxes, and heaven knows it's not one of our favorite places. Staring at those gray or brown walls while nature calls is depressing at best.

While humans willingly spend thousands of dollars to upgrade their "potty" rooms, they seem to think we'll do our business anywhere!

Now it's your turn. Brighten those necessary moments with deluxe designer litter paper liners from our supplier, *Fe-Line-De-Zine.* Each sheet is lined with bubble wrap for soft-cushioned stepping.

Easily removable adhesive backing makes changing a snap (not that it's your worry; your human will take care of that). Choose from Golden Satin (shown above), Underwater Splendor, Feline Wildlife, Abstract, or Soothing Pastel.

Abstract   Splendor   Wildlife   Pastel

Item #4445
Designer Litter Box Liners (12).........$14.95

Four-Generation Family Tree Portrait Frame
Specifically designed for felines
It's easy with this litter-friendly design

Personalized just for you!

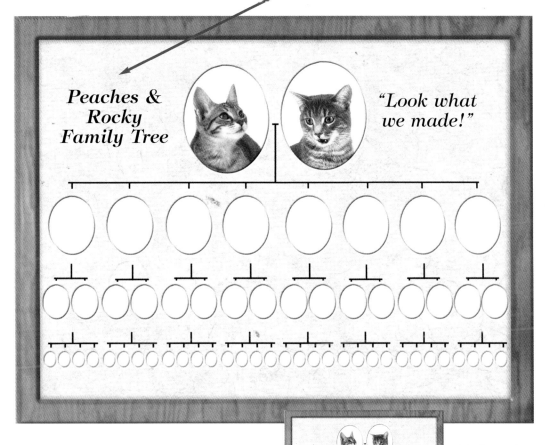

Peaches &
Rocky
Family Tree

"Look what we made!"

You're proud of your production—now you can show it off in style!

Humans, with their meager output, have it easy when creating genealogical charts or framing photographs for their family trees. But we felines know how difficult it can be, cramming those 3rd- and 4th-generation litter pics into a frame designed for humans.

It's time we had our own photograph layout, and here it is—from our friends at *Stay the Spay Foundation*. Each frame is a generous 24" x 35" with room for 62 photographs. (For those of you who are especially active, we offer the 5th Generation Extension Unit with room for 120 more!)

5th Generation extension unit. Room for 60 more!

Now there's plenty of space for all of the grandcats, great grandcats and . . .

Note: A portion of the proceeds from the sale of each of these unique frame and mat sets will be donated to the *Stay the Spay Foundation* to assist them in their goal of tripling the feline population before the end of 2006.

Item #1282 Frame & Custom Mat........................$19.95
Item #1283 5th Generation Extension Unit $12.55

Irretrievable Weights for Retrievers
It's fun to watch them struggle
They'll swim with the fishes

FLOATS REAL GOOD!

EASY TO RETRIEVE!

HUMAN NOTE: Throw This in Water for Dog!

Aren't we all just so tired of hearing how great golden retrievers and Labs are? So big deal—you throw something in the water and they bring it back. And your average cat couldn't do that if it really wanted to?

We here at *The Ultimate Cats' Catalog* know the typical retriever's flaw—they're so stupid they'll retrieve anything. So here's the best joke short of a hand grenade—the perfect way to throw a monkey wrench in their favorite aqua activity—**Irretrievable Weights**!

Try as they might they won't bring these back! And their human will once again question the relative intellectual abilities of cats and dogs.

Optional: If you think you might feel a little guilty using this product, order the "Retriever Retriever"—it might come in handy!

Each weight is imprinted clearly so the humans think they get the concept (but they never get the joke).

You wouldn't want to lift one of these so our drivers are instructed to leave them on the driveway where humans will discover them and excitedly say, *"Let's go play fetch, Fido!"*

Item #6003
Irretrievable Weights (set of two)..................$12.95
Select from: 30 lb. (to confuse them), 40 lb. (to make them suffer), 80 lb. (well, you get the picture).
Optional Retriever Retriever (see left).......................$12.99

"I'm His" Locket
Give her one—keep her true
"I belong to Blackie"

She'll love you for giving her this elegant token of your affection. And since this 24-karat locket has a place for your photo, you know she'll want to show it off to all her friends.

And at the same time you're getting bonus points for your thoughtfulness, this beautiful locket is keeping other potential suitors at bay!

Gift Wrapping Available

Buy a few and keep all of your competition away. If you're doing a lot of cattin' around, buy them by the gross!

Please submit photo (and inscription if your name isn't Blackie).

Item #7771
"I'm His" Locket...................................$12.95
Gross (144 quantity discount)..........$1,220.00

Electronic Bird Identi-Caller
You find 'em—it calls 'em
The original paw'lm computer

Insert proper card in slot and Bird Locator instantly reads bar code and emits authentic pre-recorded call.

How many times have you wasted precious minutes stalking a bird only to discover at the last minute that (a) it doesn't taste that great, (b) it's too fast to catch, or (c) it's really stalking you!

Now you can become a more efficient stalker with this great new electronic marvel. Spot your prey . . . select the proper card to learn if it's worth pursuing . . . and, if it is, simply insert the card into the slot. A push of the button and your stalking tutor emits an authentic bird call that's irresistible to the stupid little creatures.

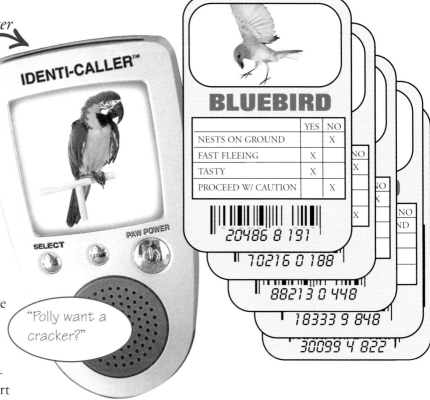

"Polly want a cracker?"

BLUEBIRD

	YES	NO
NESTS ON GROUND		X
FAST FLEEING	X	
TASTY	X	
PROCEED W/ CAUTION		X

20486 8 191
70216 0 188
88213 0 448
18333 9 848
30099 4 822

Item #9113
Electronic Identi-Caller $112.95
24 Identification Cards (wild).........................$4.95
24 Identification Cards (domesticated)..........$4.95

Cat Towels
Whisker friendly
Perfect for the puss!

Don't you just hate it when you have to use their towels? I mean when it comes to cleanliness, humans could learn a thing or two from us felines.

Insist on your own set—make it clear you won't share their spittle anymore.

Wonderfully soft and absorbent 100% Egyptian cotton (white) in a rich 600-gram weight (theirs are *Hecho en Mexico*).

Gift Wrapping Available

Item #9008 Face Towels (1 set)..........$24.95

Temperature-Controlled "Mouse Cellar"
Protects your dry-aged morsels
The perfect mouse every time

Made exclusively for us by one of France's most respected manufacturers of commercial wine cellars, this unit is a must for every gourmet cat. Keeps your meeces at the correct temperature and humidity for that perfect spur-of-the-moment snack or gourmet meal. Heavy-duty, air-tight construction assures that your mice stay fresh for months on end.

Mice lie in neat rows (facing forward) for instant visual inspection to help you select just the right morsel for just the right moment. Can be ordered in custom configurations to fit your budget and space limitations. See pricing below.

120 volts, 3225 watts.

Field Mice

Store Bought

Dry Aged

Free Range

Rare Vintage

Free Bonus!

With your purchase of any model snack cellar you will receive this FREE set of solid brass shelf-description tags. Helps you instantly spot what you're looking for!

The Connoisseur

Shelves pull out for easy access to meeces!

Truck Delivery Only

24-mouse configuration (Under the counter installation)................$319.95
48-mouse configuration (The Mini-Mouse Unit)............................$675.95
105-mouse configuration (The Gourmet)....................................$1,349.95
999-mouse configuration (The Connoisseur)...............................$1,749.95

Siamese Blue Contacts
No more Siamese envy
Frank Sinatra lives again!

Is it just us, or have you noticed how those blue-eyed Siamese get all the ohhhhs and ahhhhs?

Big deal! Blue eyes! Now any cat can have a set. And these are not just for color correction—they correct your vision too! You'll become a better stalker while looking great at the same time.

Order yours today and be a star tomorrow.

Item #1833 Blue Contacts...............$122.95

E
MEOW
MEOWM
MEOWMEOW
OWMEOWMEOWMEOWME
MEOWMEOWMEOWMEMWMEOWEOW

If you can read line 6, order prescription #6a.
If you can read line 5, order prescription #12a.
If you can read line 4, order prescription #16b.
If you can read line 3, order prescription #6a.
If you can read line 2, order prescription #16f.
If you can't read line 1, get a seeing-eye dog.

Heated, Stylish Stalking Mocs
The ultimate in hunting apparel
Keeps your paws toasty

BUY ONE PAIR—GET THE SECOND PAIR FREE!

These battery-powered heated mocs come to us straight from Italy where fashionista felines long ago discovered that style and utility are not mutually exclusive.

Now you can stalk fashionably and comfortably in this unique footwear. Hand-crafted from paw-soft, flexible yet water-proof wild wolf hides (the closest we could get to dog).

These classic boots might not help you catch bigger prey, but they're guaranteed to make stalking time (every cat's favorite moments) even more enjoyable.

No more chilly, damp paws to try your patience during those long waits for that perfect prey. When you're crouching low–silently–in those damp weeds, waiting endlessly for the perfect opportunity to pounce on that dangerous cricket, toasty warm, dry paws make all the difference in the world!

16 AAA batteries required (not included).

Gift Wrapping Available

Item #2113 Heated Stalking Mocs...................$29.95

Farewell Fido® Invisible Fence Disrupter
Get rid of annoying neighborhood dogs!
Bye-bye to barking

It's a real belly laugh to see your neighbors calling and calling for dear old Fido and trying to figure out how he got loose!

Just hide behind the nearest shrub or climb a tree and beam Farewell Fido's patented electronic signal in the general direction of your neighbor's noisy house. This amazing device instantly shuts down any electronic fence system, allowing Fido to break out and roam far and wide.

Your days will become free of annoying barking. You'll enjoy peace and tranquility while Fido is lost and confused. *Ha ha!*

Uses 2 AAA batteries (not included).

Item #6522 Farewell Fido...............$24.95

IT'S GREAT FUN!

Instant Cat/Human Translator Hat
End confusion fast!
No more human excuses

Panic Button

It's the end of the excuses for the humans—no more "Well if you wanted more food, why didn't you tell me?" Now your innermost thoughts are instantly translated into humanspeak and you'll start getting what you want.

Meow, meow, meow

Your meow	Is translated to
Meow	"Get rid of that stupid dog!"
Mee-oow	"A little lower on the tummy, please."
Me-oowwe	"Change my litter, will ya?"

Powered by an 800MHz Pet-nium chip. Panic button shuts down operation instantaneously so humans won't see thoughts not meant for them. Such as . . .

Your meow	Will not be translated to
Meee-oow-oe	"I can't believe how dumb humans are!!"

Item #4422 Translator Cap...............$19.95

Luxor®Litter
Direct from the land of our forecats
Guaranteed soft—no ifs, ands, or butts!

Our Cat Catalog worksite and sand mine, 40 kilometers north of Luxor. (We are a non-sweatshop employer.)

It was the best of times for the cat community; felines were worshiped as gods in ancient Egypt (as we should be today, but that's another story).

This ultra-dry desert blend comes to you direct from our own sand mines in Egypt for the ultimate in quality control. Softer than ordinary litter, our wind-blasted microscopic particles are more forgiving than even the finest domestic brands.

Please notify your human that this sand does not have the odor-absorbing characteristics of traditional litter, so it must be changed twice daily.

Please allow 4–6 months for delivery

Buy in quantity and save!

Truck Delivery Only

Item #8861 Luxor Litter 40 lbs. $119.95
Item #8862 Luxor Litter 80 lbs. $199.95
Item #8863 Luxor Litter 120 lbs. $309.00

Catsuit for Hairless Cats
Baby, it's cold outside!
Warm __and__ chic!

Tail Assembly Additional

We understand you wouldn't give up your classic hairless look for anything, but there are special times when a little more fur is "prefur-able."

When the temperature drops and you need a little style along with your warmth, you can't go wrong with our catsuit for comfort and style.

Subtle, well-matched zipper in front for ease of entry. Guaranteed to minus 20 degrees.

Please note: For proper care and to assure that your catsuit gives you many years of use, we recommend our Cold Fur Storage Vault (page 58).

Item #8881 Catsuit....................$29.95
Item #8882 Tail assembly............$11.95

Encyclopedia of Human Genius
Leather-bound—what a gift!
(Until they see what's inside)

Picture the joy you'll bring to your humans' face when they unwrap this elegant gift. Even though they probably haven't read a book in years, their eyes will well up with tears at your thoughtfulness.

This heirloom-quality edition features 22-karat gold accents, gilded page ends, moiré fabric end sheets, and . . . blank pages!

It might take them a minute or so, but the joke will finally dawn on them and everyone will have a good laugh! Ha ha!

And even after the brief fun is over, your gift will remain useful for years to come! We guarantee your human will proudly display these elegant tomes (out of reach of the casual browser) right alongside their unread volumes of Solzhenitsyn and Joyce.

Item #4422 Leather Book Set.........$144.95
Autographed by the author, add..........$35.00

Mounted "Fake" Canine Head
Display your kill above the hearth
Impress friends and humans with tall tales

So you didn't really bag that 110-pound giant boxer on your last safari to your neighbor's yard. Who's gonna know?

I mean, how many humans really shot that deer, elk, or bear proudly displayed above their fireplace?

Mount this unique trophy and your humans will brag, "*Yeah, my cat got that one last year,*" while you can impress your feline friends with tales of your "hunt."

100% synthetic, but our buyers couldn't believe how lifelike these heads look! You'd never know they were fake.

Imported from Korea.

Item #8866-L Mounted Labrador Head.......$49.95
Item #8866-B Mounted Boxer Head..........$69.95
Item #8866-G Mounted Shepherd Head.....$89.95
Item #8866 R Mounted Rotweiller Head.....$89.95

Combination Mouse Peeler/Fur Remover

The quick and painless way to prepare your "meeses"

Crank 'em out by the dozen!

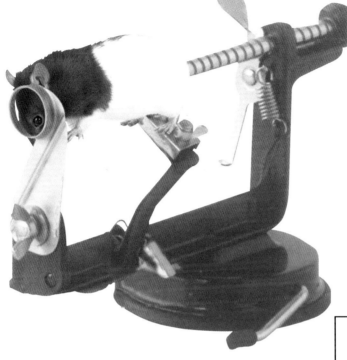

Manufacturer's warranty: 90 days or 90 mice, whichever comes first.

Gift Wrapping Available

Every cat's dream! This amazing kitchen tool skins and de-furs even the most difficult mice in just seconds. No more messy paws—no more wasting precious minutes on preparation while you could be enjoying your treats.

Pop an old Julia Child video into the VCR for a little authentic background, insert the mouse into the custom easy-hold clamp, and crank away to your heart's content. It's a gourmet experience you won't soon forget (and neither will the mouse!).

Designed to minimize "fur fly" so your kitchen stays relatively clean even after 5 or 6 "meeses" are prepared for your dining pleasure.

Invite all your feline friends over for the treat of a lifetime. You'll bask in the glow of their envious looks because you're the first on your block to own America's newest and best culinary cat kitchen appliance.

Dishwasher safe.

(Use with Snack Cellar, page 18.)

Free Bonus Gift!

Love Those Meeses to Pieces!

20 GREAT FURLESS APPETIZERS
To Please the Palate of Any Cat

With every Mouse Peeler purchase, we'll throw in this 48-page classic cookbook. A $12.95 value!

Item #4412 Mouse Peeler..................$34.95

"Cat Burglar" Lock Picking Kit
Your keys to the vault
"Here birdy, birdy"

End frustration over those locked-up tasty birdy treats. Now you'll discover where the phrase "Easy pickins'" comes from, when you take advantage of these nifty pickers. There's a tool for even the hardest lock to crack. You'll be in and out in just seconds.

They'll squawk and squawk when they see you coming with this high-quality set of tools, but they can only watch in dismay as you make quick work of their feeble "protection."

P.S. Don't forget to close the lock when you're done dining. Then you can enjoy watching your humans scratch their head in wonderment as they ponder what in the world happened to dear old Tweety.

Ladder not included.

Item #9008
22-Piece Professional Lock Picking Set............$24.95

BEFORE

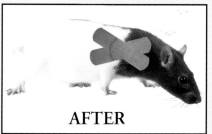

AFTER

DISCLAIMER!

No animals (almost) were hurt in any way during the production of this catalog.

Well, maybe a few meeses (especially for the—please pardon our laughter—Mouse Peeler photo shoot!) but, in general, we tried to be really nice to all of our furry friends. Before we ate them.

Chipmunks, butterflies, crickets, and other assorted creatures were all treated under the National Mail Order Catalog Guidelines for the Ethical Treatment of Animals Act, introduced into Congress by Senator Jane Fonda.

Lab Look-Alike Scratching Post
Get revenge the easy way
Scratch all day—he'll never retaliate!

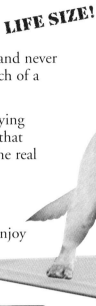

LIFE SIZE!

Go for the throat, the jugular, that tender nose and never worry about retaliation (not that a mere Lab is much of a match for you!).

Now you can keep those claws sharp while enjoying every minute! Lifelike (full size) with synthetic fur that looks so real you'll swear you're doing battle with the real thing!

Put an end to boring scratching posts and start looking forward to your daily ritual. Swipe with gusto! Live out those fantasies! Then sit back and enjoy your handiwork. We guarantee you'll find it a satisfying experience.

Colors available: Chocolate Lab, Yellow Lab, Black Lab.

Truck Delivery Only

Item #462 Lab Scratching Post..............$44.75

The Patch (No Prescription Necessary)
Don't lick that addiction—enjoy it!
Releases catnip into your system all day long.

When you simply can't break the habit and find yourself reaching for a bit of catnip at all hours of the day and night, it's time to admit defeat and order this marvel of modern medicine.

Only recently approved for over-the-counter sales by the National Association of Some Group of People, this slow-release patch delivers a constant dose of high-quality catnip *directly to your system*. Enjoy a drugged-out state for hours on end!

Based on proven flea-collar technology, but almost invisible so nobody knows you're patching but you (see available fur-matching colors). Applies in seconds. Guaranteed not to damage your fur.

Caution: For recreational use only. Do not operate heavy equipment.

Almost invisible yet keeps you smiling all day long!

Item #4522a Catnip Patch (6-month supply) $22.95
Specify white, gray, black, calico, yellow.
Item #4522b Substitute Tuna Patch...........................$22.95

Miles o' Yarn
1,287, to be exact
It's a really BIG ball!

Really, is there nothing more annoying then watching that dinky yarn ball your human gave you on your last birthday get smaller and smaller until there's nothing left to play with?

Now you can play like a kitten until you're well into your 8th life because you're never going to run out of yarn with this big fella in your toy box (or should we say, next to your toy box).

Of course you can count on your friends here at *The Ultimate Cats' Catalog* to make every one of our offerings special, and this is no exception. We're offering your choice of yarn at no additional cost (cashmere requires a slight surcharge). Select from 100% wool, hypoallergenic cotton, lush angora, pashmina, or cashmere.

Truck Delivery Only

Only color available: Multi (as shown)

Additional for cashmere: $199.00

Item #9087 Big Ball!........................$244.95

TuffCat® Plate Protector
Make a statement!
What a gift!

Next time your human's car passes a fire hydrant and some silly pooch starts chasing your wheels, these personalized license plate protectors will give them something to think about.

Your humans will love them too since they tell the world they are so intelligent (i.e., cat lovers).

Note from the editors: Personalized MEOW plate not included. We waited 6 years for this one. Get your own!

Select from: *My Other Pet Is a Cat, Don't Mess with Rexes* (for our Texas customers), or *Cats Do It in the Sand.*

Gift wrapping available.

Item #9088 Plate Protector....................$24.95

Understanding the Feline Mind
A layman's guide
Hey, we never said it would be easy!

It's our curse, but we must live with it. From our lowly desert origins, beloved by pharaohs and kings, we've evolved into the most complex of beings, difficult at best to understand.

To get the most out of our humans it's important they gain an understanding (albeit rudimentary) of how our minds work. And here's your solution. Give them this 45-volume ultimate reference guide.

This is no time for subtlety. Hide their *TV Guide*, *People*, and *National Enquirer* and then place a new volume on their nightstand every week. Before you know it (in less than a year) they'll finally start to gain an understanding of our beautiful minds.

Leather-bound, 24k gold stamping on spines.

Free Bonus!

If you share your household with a canine, our sympathies. Aside from that, we'd like to offer you this bonus as a free gift from us.

The "comprehensive" booklet *Understanding the Canine's Brain* makes a thoughtful present for your human.

Although the author was forced to add a lot of filler, it's still a full 4 pages and packed with insight.

Truck Delivery Only

Item #1709 Understanding the Feline Mind (45 volumes)..............$819.95

Nontoxic Butterfly Glue
Flap, flap, flap . . . they're stuck for good
Pick 'em up at your leisure

They're oh-so-tasty but not very filling so you have to catch dozens to get your fill. And that's a lot of work!

But you can count on the folks here at *The Ultimate Cats' Catalog* to make it easier for our feline friends. We're proud to present our patented nontoxic glue, infused with a scent butterflies find irresistible!

Simply place a drop here and there and before you know it your backyard or porch is full of the fluttery little things flapping away but going nowhere but your stomach.

Now you can take your time and "shop" at your leisure. There's no need to break a sweat. Whenever you're ready—for a snack or a meal—they'll always be waiting for you.

Item #8220
Butterfly Glue, 8 oz. $6.95

Feline Rain Repellent Spray
Keeps fur dry—and chic
No more howlin' in the rain!

You're fluffed and buffed—you're ready for a night on the town—and the forecast calls for your nemesis: RAIN!

Not to worry. Our exclusive rain repellent spreads billions of invisible bubbles on top of your fur, protecting it from the elements while keeping its natural luster. While all of your sisters are drenched and looking like wet rats (sorry for the analogy) you'll still be chic—and ever so dry!

Protein enriched so it revitalizes while it protects! Shake well.

Note: Spray a little on before you're due for your bath and drive your human crazy!

"Thanks to your Feline Rain Repellent, no more clumsy umbrella for me."

Item #2220
Feline Rain Repellent, 16 oz. $11.95

Turbocharged Petting Machine
Pets on your own schedule
Ooooh, that feels good!

For those of you with less than 100% dedicated humans, this will do the job. Now you can get all the petting you want—when you want it (and at the stroke speed that's right for you).

No need to count on the whims of your owner again. This kitty-soft hand will become your best friend!

Simply flip the switch, set the timer, and get into your favorite position.

120 volts, 45 amps

But that's not all! Order today and you'll receive . . .

Snap-On Tongue Attachment!
Tongue getting tired keeping your fur clean? Not to worry, have we got the attachment for you! Made of lifelike (as in feline-like), self-wetting, space-age materials, this little beauty will set your heart a-twitter with the very first stroke. We believe you will find the turbo boost *most* enjoyable when using this attachment.

Sells separately for $49.95!

Item #0012 Petting Machine....................$54.95

Feline-Friendly Sleep Mask/Ear Plug Set
Lightweight and easy to use
Zzzzzzzzzzzzzz

Milly, San Diego, CA

We couldn't think of a better way to tell you about these fantastic sleep/nap aids than to show you this photo our good customer Milly sent us and to share her comments with you.

"I had so much trouble trying to catch a little shut-eye because my humans have 4 smaller versions of themselves (I think the proper term is rug rats) running around making noise at all hours of the day.

*"Then I ordered your **Sleep Mask and Ear Plug Set**. Wow, what a difference! Now I get all the shut-eye I want. I'm less grouchy and I'm even nicer to those little people now, too!*

"Yours truly, Milly"

Item #8221 Sleep Mask/Ear Plug Set...........$11.95

Your Own Driver's License
The only ID you'll ever need
No age requirement

It's all about respect. Those dopey collar I.D. tags just don't cut it. I mean, without a driver's license or a credit card, you can't even cash a check!

And when you want a little Chardonnay or a sip of Veuve Clicquot you never get past the *"Can I see your I.D.?"*

Most of our customers never use this for driving a car (it's such a human thing!) but like Lucy, of Columbus, OH, said, *"You can't get into a decent singles bar without one!"*

Laminated. Available for all 50 states and all Canadian provinces. Please submit photo that doesn't look like you (so you'll be just like your human who doesn't look like herself on her driver's license either).

Available for all 50 states and all Canadian provinces.

Need a credit card too? No problem. Humans often submit applications with their pet's name and receive cards. Ask your human to apply for you. Credit card companies are unusually helpful!

Item #5566 Your Own Driver's License...........$19.95
Please indicate state

Nine Lives Tracker
Keep track of where you stand
Live wild—'till the 8th!

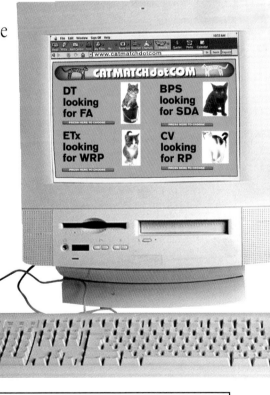

Sure we're blessed with nine lives. That's why we can live on the wild side, unlike poor humans and canines who have but one life to live. But it can be dangerous to lose track!

"Wait a minute, am I on my 6th or 7th?" you think as you tease your neighbor's Rot.

Now you can have the confidence to live recklessly and yet still be cautious as lives tick away.

Our diamond-encrusted **Nine Lives Tracker*** is as beautiful to look at as it is practical. Truly a keepsake you will cherish until the "big 9" comes along. Just stand near your tracker and its unique space-age* sensor remotely reads your body signs and "knows" (trust us) whether you are simply experiencing a scary moment, a near-death experience, or have truly lost one of your nine. Sensitivity to 10 meters.

* Based on the doomsday clock

Item #8000 Nine Lives Tracker................$11.95

Catmatchdotcom.com—Feline Dating Service

When you're curled up with your human in front of reality TV, keeping up with who's being rejected on *The Bachelor,* you probably want to ask yourself, *"What about me? Where's the perfect feline companion for me?"*

Log on to Catmatchdotcom.com and find the mate of your dream. You're just a few keystrokes away from the best years of your life.

Easy to use, feline-friendly interface lets you click on a few simple choices to get you where you want to be—and who you want to be with. Popular categories include:
• *Cattin' around* • *Long-term (2 week) relationship*
• *Wanted: small (256) family* • *Just for snuggling*

Once you've signed up, simply enter your "qualifications," e-mail a photo, and describe the type of feline friends you're looking for. Handy abbreviations shown below.

Note: Mouse not included

Abbreviation	Meaning	Abbreviation	Meaning	Abbreviation	Meaning
A	Alley cat	F	Female	Sh	Shorthair
B	Black	M	Male	T	Tiger
C	Calico	P	Pedigree	Tx	Tuxedo
D	Domestic	R	Responsible	V	Virgin
E	Exotic	S	Stud	W	Worm-free

Electric Inversion Table & Stretching Machine
Adds inches of elegant length
Won't help your abs but—woweee!—that feels good!

If you've ever seen an infomercial (and what cat hasn't—with our humans leaving us home all day with nothing to do but watch TV) then you'll instantly recognize this life-changing machine.

Simply strap in and push the automatic one-paw control and experience a gentle, controlled recline. As the blood rushes from your tail to your head, you'll immediately experience the rejuvenating effects. At the same time this amazing device applies tension, gently stretching you to a more pleasing, elongated, and thinner shape.

See dramatic results in just 10 days or your money back! (Just like on TV.) Auto-timer assures you won't get all bent out of shape.

AS SEEN O TV

6 easy payments of $19.95

Some assembly required.

Before: Note the rather "stubby" appearance, not appreciated by the opposite sex.

After: Now . . . a lean, mean fighting machine. You'll turn heads with your new lithe figure.

Item #4422
Stretching Machine............$44.95

Mr. FisherCat® Ensemble
Functional yet stylish
What all the cool cats are wearing this year

On occasion it can be embarrassing to be feline when we observe some cat's behavior, and, more importantly, their attire, as they paw crudely by the side of a stream or pond in search of a snack.

Being a feline brings with it certain responsibilities, including not only *being* good at what we do, but *looking* good as well. Raccoons fish *au naturel,* but, then, they're simply coons.

Make sure you look stylish with this great ensemble from L. L. Fishbean. Vest is waterproof, with pockets for extra minnows, which may be used as bait or for snacks. Custom cat-size pole.

Fish not included.

Item #4422
Mr. FisherCat Ensemble............$21.95

The Classic Can
Own an original!
Refurbished—but not too much

Sure it's nice to have a comfortable home—food when you want it—and a nice warm place to sleep. But admit it, you miss those cattin'-around days—meeting those old friends by the garbage can in the alley—a favorite spot to find a little friendly conversation and often a midnight snack as well.

If that's the case, you'll love our authentic, refurbished Alley Garbage Can. Our patented refurbishing process cleans the surface area thoroughly but leaves that all important aroma of each city's garbage intact! It may look new but it has that comfortable feel and smell you love.

Invite your friends over for a little gossip and conversation—just like the good-old days. And bring back the memories!

120 gal. capacity

Note: As you know, some cities have better garbage than others (from a feline's standpoint). Hence the variation in prices below.

Item #9392	The Classic Can	$44.95
Item #9392a	Brooklyn Can	$54.95
Item #9392b	Chicago Can	$34.95
Item #9392c	Chinatown (NY) Can	$124.95
Item #9392d	Chinatown (SF) Can	$134.95
Item #9392e	New Orleans Can	$172.95

Our customers say it best . . .

Unsolicited (Really) Testimonial

Dear Bruce and everyone at *The Ultimate Cats' Catalog*:

You guys are the cat's meow! I've been ordering for 3 years now and my humans have never noticed.

Good news for me! I heard Mr. Human is getting a big raise so I'm going for the Mausoleum. I've wanted it for years and now's my big chance!

Keep up the good work!

Frankie

Frankie
Trenton, NJ

CleverCat® Caps
Avoid unnecessary embarrassment
One size fits some

We know how it can feel when you live in a feline and canine household and sometimes find yourself sitting next to Butch just when your friends show up. Admit it, you're embarrassed—and for good reason!

Don't let fellow felines or even humans think you hang out with the "wrong sort." Make it clear with these clever caps that plainly say, "I'd rather be with someone else."

Unconstructed, premium, soft cotton twill caps. Low profile styling with pre-curved bill. Velcro® closure. One size fits most (yours will fit better than theirs).

Note: Dogs can't read. Tell them their cap says *"Good doggie."*

Item #3392 CleverCat® Caps (set of 2)..............$44.95

CaNN—Cat News Network
All cat news—all the time
No more Lassie reruns!

You didn't know? Of course there's a news network exclusively for us felines! You didn't think Rupert Murdock would really miss a market of 85,000,000 (and growing really fast).

For just pennies per month (billed to your human's credit card) you can keep up on all the latest feline developments. Programming for every cat—whether you're a cultured calico (Frontline Feline) or simply an alley cat (Cat-rostropic Events, CFL: Catfight League).

Monthly billing shows up as "CaNN" (we make the "a" so small they never notice).

Note: Programming only. Does not include satellite dish. No victrola trade-ins accepted.

So today!

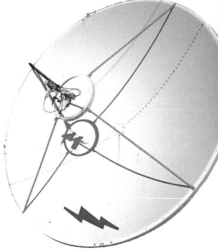

So yesterday!

Item #3392 CaNN Programming/mo........$44.95

The Ultimate Cats' Catalog
Ultimate Sleeping Environment
All the elegance you deserve—
Spare no expense!

If your human is the proud possessor of a platinum charge card, you're in luck. This is the ultimate sleeping environment and it can be all yours! Since we felines have been known to spend a few hours napping every day, a proper environment is important. And, baby, oh baby, is this the proper environment or what?

As your humans will undoubtedly be envious and will attempt to "move in" we have tastefully carved the international "No Humans Allowed" symbol into the headboard to deter them. It always works. Trust us.

BED—Solid Brazilian hardwood construction with exquisitely hand-carved appointments at both head and foot.

SHEETS—1,875-count Egyptian (of course) cotton sheets with luxurious embroidery detail inspired by classic Andalusian rugs. Flat or fitted. Sheets, pillowcases, and shams have double rows of hemstitching with Italian turnback.

BLANKETS—Our silk blankets add the ultimate crowning touch to your environment. Silk provides substantial warmth because, as we all know, natural fibers are superior. Silk charmeuse binding on all sides, mitered corners.

QUILT—120% cotton with 32 layers of soft batting. Made exclusively for *The Ultimate Cats' Catalog* in Italy where cats are not necessarily worshiped, but fine fabrics are.

PILLOWS—We added an exuberant toss of really exceptional pillows just for a little over-the-top dressing.

Machine wash sheeting; dry clean all other linen. Truck delivery (and some assembly) required.

Truck Delivery Only

Item # 9886 Sleeping Ensemble.......$12,287.95
Side tables/lamps not included

Authentic Egyptian Mausoleum
A suitable monument to your greatness
Will Fido be jealous!

BUFFY

Cat shown for size comparison only

You know your humans will never forget you when you're gone. They'll spend years dressed in mourning, wondering how they will get by without you. Face it, you are the most important thing in their life!

That's why they won't be upset when they see the somewhat large charge on their credit card statement.

"Oh well," they'll sigh, *"I can always take out a second mortgage. I guess Buffy really is worth it."*

And it's true, a feline of your stature deserves to rest in peace beneath a suitable monument. Canines can get by with a simple *"Here Lies Fido"* stone, but you're . . . well, you're a cat!

Handcrafted by Egyptian stonemasons to our exacting specifications, each mausoleum is a one-of-a-kind tribute to your greatness. Shipped by (really big) truck. Please mark preferred location because, believe us, once it's set in place, that's where it will stay.

Please specify name to be carved. 8' letters (6 letters included in price, each additional letter $487.00). Net weight 272,005 lbs. Sorry, no gift wrap available.

Truck Delivery Only

Item #3922 Mausoleum.................$217,000.95

Sigmund and Ray Poster
Original and autographed
No need to go to Vegas!

You know they're the best! If any humans understand the feline mind it's these great guys with their even greater accents and T-shirts!

This limited-edition poster will never again be available (trust us). Signed and numbered by famed artist Jo Belski, this collector's item is sure to skyrocket in value (although we can't believe you'd ever want to part with it!).

Item #3392 Autographed Poster.......................$14.95

The Original Bass-O-Matic

Saturday Night Live signature edition

Makes trout and catfish slurpies too!

You've seen it on *Saturday Night Live*—now own your own authentic copy!

We offer this limited edition SNL signature model—guaranteed to become a collector's favorite and skyrocket in value. And while you're waiting for that price appreciation you'll be enjoying the world's finest (and smoothest) seafood slurpies.

Why wait for your local convenience store to start offering slurpies for their feline clientele when you can make your own, quickly and easily? Simply drop in the fresh fish of your choice and within seconds you've got a meal fit for a cat. Built-in scale evaporator unit blasts scales into microscopic particles for ease of digestion and ease of cleaning! (Note: They never feel a thing.)

Colors available: Whitefish white, Bass black, Goldfish gold, Guppie green.

Item #4422 Bass-O-Matic.................$44.95

Glamour-Cat® Whisker Extensions

For that elegant, long-lash look

No more whisker envy!

You know the cats we're talking about—the felines who turn heads whenever they stroll into a room—the ones with the long, elegant whiskers.

Now you can have that same movie star look in just minutes. Our set of whisker extensions apply in a jiffy and come in either Alley Cat or Vamp lengths so you can get the perfect style for the mood you're in.

Your set of 24 extensions (12 Alley Cat and 12 Vamp) arrive in a handy acrylic storage case. Your choice of standard whisker colors: black or white. Or, for that fabulous night on the town, select from our exclusive neon colors: magenta, blue, or green. Please specify color when ordering.

Gift Wrapping Available

Item #5583 Whisker Extensions...........$9.95

Henna Stencil Cattoos

Fur friendly

You're hot—get hotter!

You're a cat so it's understood that you're exotic already but that doesn't mean you can't create an even more exotic (and erotic) look for yourself. And these ever-so-trendy Henna Cattoos are just the ticket.

This 6,000-year-old art form of temporary furpainting with henna has finally reached the North American feline community and our customers are clamoring for them! Designs are temporary (they last 2 to 4 weeks) and are lick-resistant so you won't inadvertently disturb your work of art.

Our set includes all-natural products: fur preparation gel, henna powders, eucalyptus oil, removable stencils, and complete instruction booklet.

Select from Traditional Asian Stencils (including Hsun-Tao designs and the complete Yao Min series) or Modern American Stencils (including the trendy, celebrity barbed-wire look and the ever-popular butterfly).

Item #2220
Asian Cattoo Stencils...........................$6.96
American Cattoo Stencils.....................$7.95

Charms Galore Charm Necklace

Lots of litters? No problem . . .

Buy these charms by the gross!

We've heard from many of our customers who have tried to modify a human charm bracelet for feline use. And the complaint is always the same: not enough hanging room to showcase their brood!

So we had one of America's most respected jewelers create this special maxi-attachment necklace with more than enough room for all the charms you'll need.

Lightweight construction assures even the most prolific moms can carry the load (necklace holds up to 247 charms).

Gift Wrapping Available

Item #1882
Charm Necklace...............................$22.95
Charms, per dozen............................$15.75

The Eliminator!

When everything else fails

"I'll be back!"

As you know, the editorial board here at *The Ultimate Cats' Catalog* supports being nice to canines (whenever possible) as well as other creatures of lesser intelligence. But there can come a time in any cat's life—especially if it's number 8—when enough is enough and nothing but extreme measures will do.

If you're a 4-pound weakling and some Tom kicks cat litter in your face, what do you do?

For sticky situations like this we can heartily recommend the ultimate in sticky (napalm) solutions: **The Eliminator**, by *Gone-in-a-Flash Products Corp.*

The fun begins when you show up pulling your Eliminator and see the look in their eyes. *"Maybe I've gone too far,"* they think, but it's too late for regrets.

Simply set the proper temperature and pull the trigger. Whoosh! Fido is gone in a flash! It's painless (trust us).

No need to get within striking range of those snapping jaws—our **Eliminator** has a flame-throwing range of over 60 feet! Convenient temperature control settings (see recommendations below right). Adjustable shoulder strap.

Note: Hazardous materials permit required for operation.

Not Much Left!

"I'm sending a photo of all that's left of Baron. I give a "2 claws up" rating to your Eliminator."

—*Peetie, Detroit*

DANGER
HIGHLY FLAMMABLE

Truck Delivery Only

Optimum Temperature	Optimum Dog
100–250 degrees	Pugs (and bugs)
250–450 degrees	Miniature yorkies
450–600 degrees	Poodles (small)
600–850 degrees	Retrievers/shepherds
850–999 degrees	Rotts
Over 1,000 degrees	Determined pit bulls

Item #3552 The Eliminator.........................$256.95
Extra napalm (store in cool, dry place).........$18.95

Lazy Cat's Bushel of Fake Mice
Turn 'em in for treats
No more hunting, ever!

Remember when you were a kitten? The thrill of the hunt and the kill --- and every time you brought home a trophy you got a treat?

Now that you've gotten older, you don't want to work so hard (and you know you'll get the treats anyway).

But now you can keep your humans happy because they'll think you're still a great mouser and you won't have to break a sweat. These fake (but amazingly realistic) mice will fool even the most observant human.

Just reach in and grab one every time you're feeling unappreciated (or hungry), and after the initial shriek, get ready for the praise: *"Another one?! I'm glad you're on the job!"* You get the praise and the treats, without the work.

Also, it's great fun to watch the humans hold them by their plastic tails and drop them in the trash.

Item #2320
Bushel of Fake Mice...................$21.95

100% brass hinges for quick, quiet, deadly operation.

Trapdoor Birdhouse
Get'em while they snooze!
No assembly required

They approach unaware . . . landing lightly on their perch and hopping quickly inside. Coming home after a long day's work (eating worms!) and planning on settling down to a nice nap.

Wham! *"What's going on?"* they think, as the bottom of their abode drops out and they tumble into your eager, warm paws.

The patented, quick-release mechanism assures that even the most quick-witted birdies won't be able to get their wings flapping until it's much too late!

Note: It's so much fun, some cats release them and do it all over again!

Item #1120
Trapdoor Birdhouse............................$34.95
Mounting hardware and 5' pole included

Subliminal Message Treat CDs
They'll be your slave
A real treat (if you get our drift)

You've heard it said time and time again: "You can't teach an old human new tricks." But these proven subliminal message tapes will put an end to that myth!

Want more treats? More toys? More lovin'? Now you can get all you need. Your humans won't know why they are suddenly in such a mood to do your bidding. They can't hear the millisecond bursts of subliminal messages inserted in these tapes. You don't care how it works, just so that it does!

Excerpts—

Tape #1 Classic Stories—More Treats: "It was the best (treats, treats) of times, it was (treats, treats) the worst of (treats) times . . ."

Tape #2 Detective Stories—More Toys: "Okay, wise guy (more toys, toys), hand over (toys) the rod (more toys, toys), I know you're packing (toys, toys) . . ."

Tape #3 Romance Stories—More Petting: "As he held her (more lovin') in his embrace (more pettin', more lovin'), her lips (more lovin', lovin') parted in (more lovin') anticipation . . ."

Have them gift wrapped and send as a birthday present so they won't get suspicious. They'll love you for your thoughtfulness!

Item #1003
Subliminal CDs (3)..................$24.95

Editorial
Be Nice to Canines (Really).

Huh...

Being felines ourselves, we can understand how easy it can be to observe the common canine and feel an unrelenting surge of superiority. The dopey look, the hanging tongue, the clumsiness . . .

Although out catalog does feature a number of items that enable you to ridicule, harass, or even dispense with canine pests, we do ask for your restraint. They are, after all, well . . . creatures.

Remember, be nice to them when you can. It's not their fault they were born dogs.

Population-Bomb Pills
Spay reversal made fun and easy
Pregnant in a week or your money back!

You've been through the pain . . . you've been through the humiliation . . . you've been fixed. And you're not happy about it one bit. You'll never again be able to pass your genes on to hundreds more offspring.

Just who are those humans to tell us we don't have the God-given right to procreate?

Now you can fix them with our guaranteed spay-reversal pill. Works quickly and easily through the miracle of modern medicine (trust us). One pill once a day for just 6 days and you're back in business. Humans never catch on. It's fun to watch their confusion when faced with yet another litter. *"Look how wonderful Bootie is— she's nursing someone else's babies. They couldn't be hers because . . ."*

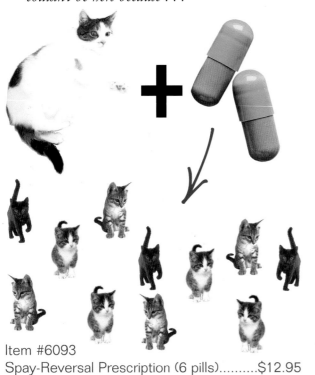

Item #6093
Spay-Reversal Prescription (6 pills).........$12.95

Feline's Favorite Flannels
Back flap litter access
Yes, they really fit!

Our **CRAZY** Low Price
NOW $22.95

We gave our buyer (who used to work for J. Peterman) a bonus for spotting these in Hong Kong just as they were about to be destroyed. Rejected by a major mail-order clothier (because the manufacturer's computerized sewing machines ran amok and turned out 2,000 sets unsuitable for humans), they're perfectly tailored—sort of—for the average feline. Sleeves roll up easily if the fit isn't perfect.

Button front and rear flap for easy litter-box accessibility. Army red only. Non-returnable.

Especially useful for you felines who order our inversion machine. See page 32.

Item #1113
Feline's Favorite Flannels.................$22.95
X Long, XX Long, XXX Long only

Breakfast Vita-Juicer

Vitamin M for the healthy cat

Squeeze your own!

Cat-friendly crushing (er, we mean "activation") chain.

Stainless-steel fittings for strength and durability

Easy to empty fur filter

Feeling listless? Run down even as the day begins? Of course you are! You're not getting enough vitamin M.

For that perfect morning wake me up—one that's chock-full of that one important vitamin you need most to get you off to a fast start, there's an easy way—and you're looking at it!

Pop in a mouse, pull the chain (hard), and watch as your glass fills instantly with pure nectar.

Mice—you gotta love 'em. They're great hot, cold, fried, aged, and as you'll happily discover, in liquid form as well.

Can also be used with other tasty, furry critters.* Results may vary.

*You'll get great taste but no vitamin M.

Gift Wrapping Available

The Secret of Vitamin M

Most vitamins are formulated to release slowly into your bloodstream to provide energy all day long. This, of course, would simply not do for the average feline, who needs to slow down frequently for naps.

Scientists have discovered, however, that vitamin M (available only from freshly pressed meeses) provides a powerful boost that lasts less than an hour. That's plenty of time for a short frolic with a toy or a brief romp in the yard. And when nap time calls, you'll be ready. Trust us.

Item #9992 Breakfast Vita-Juicer......................$44.95

"My Cat's the Best" Award Ribbon Set
Feed their ego, not yours

They'll brag and brag and brag

We all know that cats don't suffer from low self-esteem. But humans do, and these elegant ribbons will help make them more proud of you.

There's a ribbon guaranteed to give your humans the reinforcement they need so their hearts will swell with pride (as if just having you around isn't enough!).

Select from our most popular stock ribbons, create your own award or, better yet, get the entire set.

Select from:	
Best Mouser	Best Fur
Most Beautiful	Best in Litter
	Miss Congeniality

Customized ribbons (whatever you want your award to say) are also available.

Item #6068
Individual Ribbons......................$4.95
Add your own text....................$14.95
Set of 4 stock ribbons............$21.95

Earn Reward Points!
You've been approved. And there's no limit!
Go to town

We imprint your human's credit card number here

And when we say rewards—we mean rewards! Now every time you make a purchase from *The Ultimate Cats' Catalog* we keep track of your dollar totals and in a short period of time you'll be eligible for free merchandise!

We've selected our most popular items to offer as rewards, from **Feline Rain Repellent** to the ultimate: **The Connoisseur's Mouse Cellar** (you'll have to stock it yourself).

So push your human's limit to the limit and earn those rewards you so richly deserve!

When you reach this amount	You're eligible to receive this free gift
$100	Calendar, pg. 13
$500	Rain Repellent, pg. 28
$1,000	Tail Ring, pg. 12
$5,000	Towels, pg. 17
$10,000	Chipmunker (next page)
$25,000	Eliminator, pg. 39
$100,000	Connoisseur's Cellar, pg. 18

Call today to sign up! Our operators are always on duty.

Chipmunker®
Pop 'em in—pop 'em out!
A cold weather treat

Yeah, they're cute, but they're stupid and destructive and that's why your humans don't get too upset when we move in for the kill on a nice chipmunk youngin'.

But why just toss them playfully in the air and discard them when they stop moving? Discover what gourmet cats have long known: Toasted baby chipmunks on a bun are a delicacy that's hard to beat!

And now they're easy to prepare as well, with our patented Chimpmunker. Just pop 'em in and they're ready in seconds. Cooks by electromagnetic pulses to eliminate that annoying "fur singe" problem. And it's battery powered so you can take it along to your favorite hunting grounds and enjoy your treat right on the spot! UL approved.

Batteries and mustard not included.

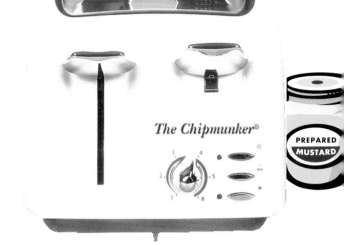

Your toaster just won't do! Note the chipmunk-sized round holes.

BATTERY POWERED!

The Chipmunker®

PREPARED MUSTARD

Item #7800
Chipmunker..........................$34.95

Personalized Christmas Stocking Set
Monopolize the gifts
No place to put them but in your stockings!

Easily confused, humans can be tricked into giving you all the prezzies during the holidays.

When Fido wipes the sleep from his eyes and discovers Santa left everything for you, we guarantee he'll crawl off feeling unloved.

This set of five Christmas stockings comes embroidered with your name on each one, leaving no doubt as to who gets the gifts.

Embroidery maximum: 12 letters. Select typeface:

Snuggles (sans serif) *Fluffy* (script)

Your name on every one!

Your Name Here · And Here · And Here · And Here · And Here

Item #1882
Christmas Stockings (set of 5)..............$22.95

Furball Sculpture Kit
Time to show your creativity
Bend it, shape it—any way you want it!

Tired of seeing all of your hard work go down the drain? Why cough it up only to see it scooped up and disposed of? It's time to recycle!

Our exclusive forms help you to create true works of art from those seemingly useless furballs. Just fill the nonstick form of your choice, let harden overnight . . . and your one-of-a-kind sculpture pops out easily, ready for painting and decorating.

Everyone is guaranteed to be impressed with your creativity, eliciting comments like *"Why can't dogs be so clever?!"* Your human will cherish your artwork equally with their kid's report cards and elegant "refrigerator art."

Select from the all-time favorite form designs shown above.

The painted and decorated examples shown above are compliments of Furball in our shipping department.

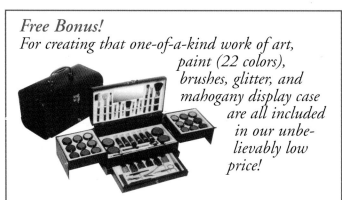

Free Bonus!
For creating that one-of-a-kind work of art, paint (22 colors), brushes, glitter, and mahogany display case are all included in our unbelievably low price!

Furball Sculpture Kit (Select designs)
Item #2282	Eiffel Tower	$9.95
Item #2283	Big Ben	$9.95
Item #2284	U.S. Capitol	$9.95
Item #2285	Golden Gate Bridge	$9.95
Item #2285	Leaning Tower of Pisa	$9.95

Unsolicited Testimonial

"I *love* your catalog!"
You guys are great! I get all my gift shopping done with one simple phone call. Keep up the good work!

—*Whizzer, Boise, ID*

TurboNail® Polisher/Sharpener
Keep your "weapons" in tip-top shape
Razor sharp in half the time!

There's a juicy little critter scurrying across the kitchen floor, but drat! You've neglected that pedicure—your nails are chipped and dull. They may be capable of killin' that critter, but you really won't look good doing it.

Now all it takes is a few seconds to keep your nails in fighting form. The TurboNail® is the fastest claw polisher/sharpener on the market today. Your claws will always be buffed and honed to razor-sharp perfection. Features one wheel for buffing, one for honing, and one for sharpening. Easy paw-touch controls.

And to complete the look, apply some of our exclusive Ultimate nail polish (see page 13).

Guaranteed: a perfect finish for the well-heeled cat.

Item #1882
TurboNail.............................$22.95

Fang Whitener
No more yellow
Look sharp—get more dates!

Easy-pour cap makes whitening easy!

It's all that garbage food they give us! Soft and mushy, it sticks in the cracks and crevices of our teeth, causing decay and that unsightly yellowing. Of course that occasional mouse doesn't help either.

If there's one thing that will turn off that cute little Siamese you've been padding after, it's yellow fangs. But one drop of this amazing stuff in your water dish every day and you'll be smiling with confidence again.

Instructions are right on the label. Simply leave by your water dish and your human should be smart enough to figure out what to do. One hopes.

Before ☞

☜ **After**

CATS PRIDE
FANG
WHITENER
100 ml (3.3 fl. oz.)
SHINE AND SPARKLE FOR HER!

Item #0882   Fang Whitener, 6 oz. $12.95

Your Puss on the Puerina* Box
Superstar status!
Your 15 minutes of fame

Humans can aspire to get their mug on the Wheaties® box à la Tiger Woods and Mary Lou Retton, but that's nothing compared to our exclusive offering.

We've contracted with the world's largest purveyor of premium feline chow to allow our customers' pusses to adorn these special commemorative boxes!

Your pix

Your friends will be suitably impressed with your new-found fame and so will your humans (not that it matters). Please include photo (nonreturnable).

* Not to be confused with that other brand of cat food

Your box!

Item #0012 Puss on Puerina...............$2,112.00
(4 million box distribution)

Real Live Human Pet
Turn the tables—own your own!
They're so cute and playful

Please select male or female

Yes, it's true, we felines laugh behind the backs of our humans whenever they say, "*I own a cat.*" (It generally takes humans years to realize who's really in control . . . who really owns whom.)

But now you really can own one (a human, that is). They're somewhat easy to train and they provide a boatful of laughs.

Potty training can be a problem (get some of that "anticlumping" litter) but they can be fun to show off to your feline friends. Buy them a Hermès® collar, dress them up in silly costumes, and take them for a walk—now it's your turn to aggravate them!

The next time your friends complain that their humans don't treat them right, you can say, "Why not adopt one of your own? They make great pets and then *you* can call the shots!"

Sorry—no gift wrapping available on these items.

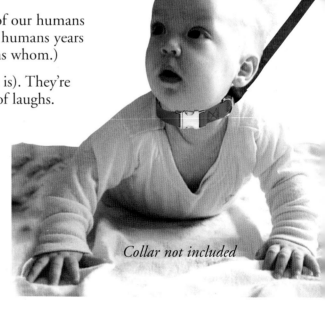
Collar not included

Delivery notes: Truck shipment only. Please have human carrier on hand. We guarantee live delivery.

Item #7800 Human (Male).................$177.95
Item #7801 Human (Female)............$197.95

Canine Claw Necklace
Impress friends—intimidate foes
"Wow—you killed that?!"

Tired of that pit bull pushing you around? *Don't get no respect?* Here's a way to make every dog think twice before fooling around with you.

Our authentic (not only authentic *looking* but really authentic) canine claw necklace says, *"I'm rough, I'm tough—look what I bagged last week!"* Guaranteed* to solve all your canine bully problems.

And when the feline mating season rolls around (did it ever leave?) you'll get all the girls with this macho look (trust us).

* In the unlikely event that our Canine Claws doesn't do the job, see our Eliminator, page 39.

Item #9012 Claw Necklace $72.00

Cat's-Request® Electronic Sign
Easy to program
No need to be subtle!

...FOR LUNCH PLEASE HAVE FRESH CREAM AVAILABLE... TONIGHT I SHALL BE REQUESTING TUNA TARTARE... AND FOR DESSERT...

CAT'S REQUEST™

Deep down, humans want to give in to our every desire. But they're only, well . . . they're only human and often times they slip up and forget.

That's why they will welcome this handy electronic marvel in their kitchen. *"It's about time!"* they'll exclaim with delight, *"Now I can be absolutely sure Blackie gets whatever his little heart desires at every meal!"*

Easily programmable, your dining request scrolls constantly across the screen all day long, acting as an impossible-to-miss reminder of your desires.

And when you tire of listing your culinary requests you can start demanding (oops, we mean requesting) other goods and services you may require.

Truck Delivery Only

Special feature: There's a button on the front panel that reads "Stop Scrolling!" but we've made arrangements with the manufacturer to have it disconnected. Your requests shall *not* be denied!

Item #7772 Cat's-Request Sign...............$112.00

Big Beautiful Cats Pin-up Calendar

They're hot, they're sexy . . . they're naked!

Every feline's fantasy

If you're offended (as we are) by those cheesecake calendars your humans tend to display . . . if you've seen enough Pamela Anderson to last a lifetime . . . here's something to get your heart a-pumpin'.

Who wants to see all that *skin!* If it's fur you're looking for, this is the calendar of your dreams. It's a full year's worth of raw, sensuous energy—the biggest, baddest, and most beautiful cats on the planet.

Oooh, those long, sharp claws . . . the bulging muscles, the powerful jaws . . . we get weak-kneed just thinking of what the next month will bring!

Available in either PG-13 or R rated* editions. Please specify.

*Must be 3 years or older to order. Adult signature required for delivery

Item #2220 Big Beautiful Cats Calendar
PG-13 Edition..$6.95
R rated Edition.....................................$16.95

Can you e-mail your order?
Of course you can!
Just dial up and have fun!

"I'm not very good with the telephone touchpad but I'm a whiz with a mouse! I love your Web site and online ordering service."
—*Buckaroo, Athens, GA*

www.ultimatecatscatalog.com

Also on our web site:

✔ *Product reviews (from our loyal customers like you)*

✔ *Testimonials (find out what others like best about our stuff)*

✔ *Customer complaints (really)*

Insta-Snack Vending Machine Route
Make big bucks in your spare time
Perfect for the cat-trepeneur

Here's the financial independence you've been looking for. One of America's fastest growing franchises, *Tiny Parts® Vending Machines,* has territories open in *your* home town!

No more begging for treats or toys. Now you'll have all the pocket money you want—and more. It's easy and there's (almost) no risk! Simply place your machines in locations where fellow felines congregate and you're on your way to untold wealth.

Send for your free video today and learn how others have changed their lives the *Tiny Parts* way!

It may seem outlandish to think you can get filthy rich without working very hard* but we've got thousands of *Tiny Parts* franchisees worldwide who, because of the big bonus we paid them (whoops, we mean out of the goodness of their hearts) are willing to vouch for our claims.

TINY PARTS CORP.™ **Mousie Parts**

TINY PARTS CORP.™ **Tuna Pieces**

FOR CATS ONLY   FOR CATS ONLY

Initial start-up includes:
- 2 Tiny Parts machines
- 40 lb. bag of tuna parts
- 40 lb. bag of mousie parts
- Heavy canvas bag to hold your "loot"
- License agreement
- "How to Get Your Vendor's License" Booklet
- Prospectus for 4 Paws Feline Fund (to help you invest your newfound wealth)

$$$$$$$$$$ $$$$$$$$$

●**Territories available. Act fast!**

"I started out with just 12 Tiny Parts dispensers and now my route has grown to 872 locations! Thanks to you I'm the richest cat on my block!"
—*Peetie, Brooklyn, NY*

* Just because humans fall for these deals all the time doesn't mean this one isn't legit.

Item #8875 Tiny Parts Franchise
Start-up fee and supplies......................$1,688.95

The 4 Paws Feline Fund
Support feline-friendly companies
No dogs in this portfolio!

You're torn between building a nice nest egg and using your money to support feline friendly companies. It's not easy when you have to do all that research yourself—all those charts and graphs!—and who trusts stockbrokers these days!?

Trying to find time for stock research and still fit in that all important nap and play time can be stressful.

Well, no need to cough up a furball. The crack team of financial analysts at **The 4 Paws Feline Fund** (and you *can* trust them) have put together a fund that can double or triple your investment overnight—at the same time you're getting a good night's sleep.

Invest safe and secure today and enjoy a comfortable retirement.

RECOMMENDED BY THE MARKET SAVVY CATS AT THE ULTIMATE CATS' CATALOG

At any given time, your portfolio may include such feline-friendly stocks* as:

- Petco
- Cat
- Ford (they own Jaguar)
- Kittykitty.com
- Microsoft (they sell mice)
- Purina

* *No Korean stocks*

How to order . . .

Simply paw in your human's credit card number (see order form for instructions) and the amount you wish to be deducted every month.

Deductions will be shown on your human's statement as "pay per view" so they'll be none the wiser.

For a free prospectus, write c/o *The Ultimate Cats' Catalog.*

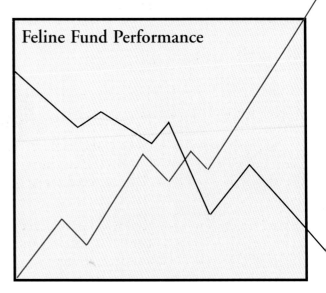

Feline Fund Performance

5 year performance vs. Dogs of the Dow
_____ 4 Paws Fund
_____ Dogs of the Dow

Wrat Wraps*
South of the border treat
Real Tijuana wrats!

As a cultivated cat you've enjoyed sushi from Japan and Croque Mouse-eurs from France (see page 11). Now it's time to experience the new taste sensation that's sweeping the nation (or at least the homes of cats with foodie humans).

You simply can't make these at home. Real chefs know the secret is not in the wraps. There are a few regional variations, of course, but basically, a wrap is a wrap. No, the real secret is in the filling. You'll never find more tasty or tender wrats than those wandering the streets and back alleys of Tijuana, where this speciality originated.

And that's exactly what you get—shipped in dry ice for full flavor protection—direct from old Mexico!

Our exclusive supplier, the It's a Wrap Corporation, catches their supply daily and before the big, fat critters know what's happening, they're run through a patented 42-step tenderizing process, wrapped, packed, and flash-frozen. This is a treat that shouldn't be missed. Trust us. Hot dipping sauce included.

Editor's note: Please do not leave these things sitting out on the kitchen counter where a human may happen upon them. Our customers report that, upon discovering what they have eaten, humans tend to throw up rather quickly. There's absolutely no accounting for taste!

* Not to be confused with the more common RatWraps found in every local pet supply store.

Item #1110 Wrat Wraps (6)...............$16.95

ScaryCat Bedtime Tails
Translated from the original
Makes your fur stand on end

Humans read to help them drift off to sleep. Felines read for enjoyment and intellectual stimulation, since we have no need for sleep inducers.

And here's a bedtime reading collection you will really enjoy. Translated from the original text by Pretty Boy, these scary stories read better than the originals! We guarantee your fur will stand on end or your money back.

Including:
"The Cats of Ulthar," Lovecraft
"House of 7 Greyhounds," Hawthorne
"The Telltail Heart," Poe

"The Black Cat," Poe
"Rats," James
And many more!

Item #9902 ScaryCat Bedtime Collection, PG-13 Edition..........$6.95
R rated Edition.........................$9.95

Dog/Cat I.Q. Tester
Put them to shame
No tricks necessary

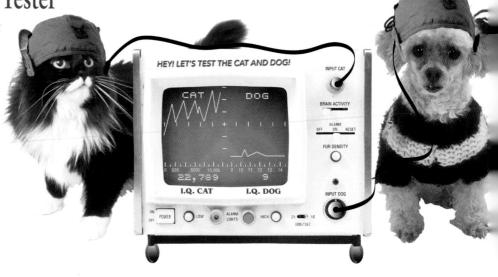

Tired of your neighbor's pooch getting all the attention? Especially for something stupid like shaking hands? Well, simply show up with our handy portable Dog/Cat Intelligence Tester and set the record straight. They'll gasp at the results but it won't be a surprise to you!

Then watch as Fido wanders pitifully from human to human trying to shake while you're basking in the limelight!

Hard to miss front panel sign prompts humans to put it to use instantly. Instant electronic LED readout proves your point once and for all. It's great fun. Use it over and over again!

Batteries not included.

Item #9392 Dog/Cat I.Q. Tester...................$34.95

Virtual Environment Goggles
3-D scenery
So that's what it's like!

Thinking of running away from home? Bored with your environment and looking for a change? Well, before you make any rash decisions, find out how the other half really lives.

If you're a city cat stuck on the 4th-floor penthouse—or a country cat bored with looking at nothing but fields and trees—now it's possible to "test drive" a new environment with these Virtual Environment Goggles.

Full motion video. Playing time 120 minutes. 1280 x 1280 resolution.

Urban View

Country View

Item #9198 Virtual Environment Goggles................$34.95

Humi-Beenies
Collect 'em all
Watch your investment soar!

You've seen 'em on TV, you've seen 'em on eBay. They're the world's greatest investment since Internet stocks.

They're cute, they're adorable, and they're based on real human characters you run into every day.

Buy one or the entire set of Humi-Beenies but order now because these limited (trust us) editions will sell out fast!

Dishwasher safe. Gift wrapping available.

Next releases—Coming in our next catalog: Harriet Housewife, Pete the Pilot, Billy Bad Boy, Cheryl Cheerleader.

Rodney Redneck
Rodney Redneck lives in a shack,
Has a tattoo of a dog on his back.
Goes fishin' in summer,
In fall he shoots deer,
A good time to him
Is a six-pack of beer.

Sally Stewardess
Sally the Stewardess flies in the air.
You want your beverage?
She doesn't care.
The flight is real bumpy,
You think you will die,
And all she can say when you leave
Is bu-bye!

Farmer Frank
Frank is a farmer, grows turnips and corn.
Never been out of the town
Where he's born.
Raises some chickens and a few cows
And on his day off he goes out and
He plows.

"Send me the entire set!"

"I spotted a good condition Harriet Housewife when I was perusing the neighbor's trash for some possible fish heads. Wow! What a find! I immediately sold it on eBay for $12,500. I'm hooked now. Send me the entire set."

—*Bootsey, Iowa City, IA*

Guaranteed Price Appreciation

We absolutely guarantee your Humi-Beenies will soar in value* or your money cheerfully refunded.

*Or they will provide hours of clawing and batting-around fun.

Item #4412   Rodney Redneck....................$4.95
Item #4413   Farmer Frank...........................$4.95
Item #4414   Sally Stewardess.....................$4.95

Feline Yellow Pages
Let your paws do the walking
Now available in your area

Sometimes it's difficult to be feline in a human-centric world. Fortunately, you have *The Ultimate Cats' Catalog* for all the products you need, but where do you go for local services? Which taverns will let you belly up to the bar? Which are the best dry (fur) cleaners? Which restaurants offer take-out, no questions asked, with your human's credit card?

The Ultimate Cats' Catalog has recently entered into an exclusive publishing agreement with FelineFinder, the famous Feline Yellow Pages people. After years of meticulous research, FelineFinder is rolling out these special editions to major metropolitan areas around the country. As you will see below, we've also arranged a special low price for our good customers like you.

To order, simply enter your 5 digit Zip code to receive the correct edition for your area.

Now available in
- New York
- Chicago
- Tuscaloosa
- Los Angeles
- Atlanta

Item #4400 Feline Yellow Pages................$6.95

Tabletop Crawfish Factory
Fresh and tasty
Your never-ending supply

It doesn't matter whether you say Crah-fish or Cray-fish, they're just as tasty either way and this must-have item will provide you with all you need—with a convenience that can't be matched.

Made for us exclusively by the All You Can Eat Corporation. Their tabletop units are renowned for their super-oxygenation units, which help you crank out the crawfish almost as fast as you can eat them! Features a patented, double air lock "Paw Porthole" unit for easy access. No need to get your paws wet!

Table-size unit can fit easily where the aquarium used to be before you ate all the goldfish and your humans gave up having (live) fish around the house (it was a silly idea anyway).

Item #9008 Crawfish Factory....................$67.95

Tuna Intervention Program
Get that tuna off your back
You know it's time!

There comes a time in every feline's life when they must face facts and admit it: They're hooked. Tuna addiction may seem innocuous but it can lead to depression, loss of self-esteem, and even a life of crime (see below).

Perhaps you have a friend or member of the family who is beginning to display the telltale signs. Don't delay. Act now, before it's too late—throw a tuna intervention gathering and help them help themselves! We know you're busy, so our complete kit has everything you need!

Included:

- 36 creative yet sympathetic invitations (guaranteed to bring a crowd)
- Pithy inspirational sayings to help give support, i.e., "You can do it!"
- 24-hour hotline, 1-800-NOMORETUNA
- Motivational cassettes let them listen to heartwarming stories of how others broke the habit

"I was stealing to feed my habit!"

"It's true, I was using my human's credit card to run up horrendous charges every month at Tuna-R-Us.com.

"At first I was angry when my friends threw me a tuna intervention party but now I've seen the light—no more tuna for me!"

—*Fraidy, Billings, MT*

Item #7009 Tuna Intervention Program.................$79.50

Cold Fur Vault
Reenergize your coat
It's in the vault!

It's a fact of life. As we age our coats get dull and lose their luster. Our fur just doesn't have the same sheen and body as when we were young. Remember how fluffy and soft your fur was when you were a kitten?

Our Brrr-Fur Cold Storage Vault & Fur Reenergizer is your ticket to long-lasting care of your coat. No need to haul your fur down to the vault like humans do. This unit is available 24/7. Just climb inside and take a cat nap while this amazing machine does its work.

Remember, caring for your coat is a lifetime commitment. Pop inside every day or so and you'll look healthier, younger, and more attractive. Your friends will be begging like dogs to know your secret!

Features precision temperature control and inside quick-release safety latch. Works amazingly well with our Catsuit (see page 21).

Item #9223 Brrr Fur Vault......................$99.50

Cricket Fry-Boy
Pop 'em in—pop 'em out!
A cold-weather treat

Merrily they go hopping by. Then comes the pounce —you've caught one—and another, and another and another! They're so easy to catch you pile them up by the dozen. But then what?

We all know they don't really taste that great raw. Those legs with all those jumping muscles are difficult to chew, much less digest!

Well, here's your answer. After intense competition with George Foreman we were able to win the U.S. rights to distribute the next hot kitchen appliance: the Cricket Fry Boy, from Hop Right In Inc.

It's fun! Just toss 'em into the boiling oil and fish them out when they're crispy. Six handy cricket-size skewers included.

Item #0009 Cricket Fry-Boy.........$44.50

Power Litter Lifter
Don't just cover—create!
Makes pooping fun again

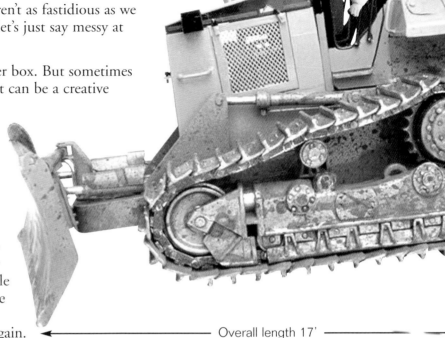

It's annoying. Humans just aren't as fastidious as we are and the results can be, well, let's just say messy at times.

Sure they'll clean out our litter box. But sometimes that can take the fun out of what can be a creative exercise.

This half size working model of that famous earth-mover they named after us is authentic down to the smallest detail (tiny little pistons go up and down, up and down).

You'll no longer be limited to the basic paw, paw, paw to cover those tiny piles. Now you can pile your sand high, build a berm, create hills and valleys—then tear everything down and start over again. It's fun—it's creatively challenging!

Overall length 17'

So grab your lunch box, don your hard hat, and entertain yourself!

Minor note: You will need this somewhat larger litter box to enjoy this item. Special order; please call for price.

Overall length 47'

Truck Delivery Only

Item #4456 Power Litter Lifter......................$22,712.95

BogieCat® Trench Coat Ensemble
Retro but hip
Here's lookin' at you, babe!

CLEARANCE
WAS $ 107.95
NOW
$ **7.95**
LIMITED QUANTITIES

It was twilight—we were wandering the back streets of Casablanca, looking for trouble.

The smoke-filled bars we visited were jammed with serious-looking women and more than enough men, all fashionably dressed in '50s trench coats and smoking foul-smelling cigarettes.

It seemed like "As Time Goes By" was playing in every establishment and we found ourselves expecting Bogie to appear at any moment.

After a few (one is too many) absinthes, our minds were sufficiently foggy and we decided we had hit upon the newest fashion statement for smart cats everywhere.

Everything after that is lost in a mist reminiscent of the clouds of cigarette smoke that surrounded us.

Late the following morning, as the sun streamed far too aggressively into our shabby hotel-room window, there, on the nightstand, amid a few leftover coins and a crumpled cigarette pack, was *the document*.

It was a contract we had apparently signed the previous evening for 1,000 units of the trench coats and hats.

With the above tale as our disclosure, we hereby list this item for your consideration at a price we feel adequately reflects our dubious judgment.

We highly recommend an absinthe (or two) while you are considering your decision to order.

Unique "North African" natural shoulders

Atlas mountain goat bone buttons

Hem (sort of)

In the unlikely event you would like to send this as a gift, gift wrapping is available.

Item #1709 Trench Coat Ensemble...........$7.95

Hot-Air Balloon Hook
It's a one-way trip
Bye-bye, Butch!

Our longtime customers often write in to say we don't offer enough "Be nasty to the dog" items. So here you have our newest creation: The Deluxe Hot-Air Balloon Hook!

It looks innocuous enough, lying there on the ground. And the affixed bait (ooops, we mean doggie treat) lures the hapless canine into thinking they've discovered a tasty morsel.

But *wham!* once they get within 2 feet of the hook, its powerful magnetic field takes over and latches onto the poor dog's collar. Afraid of heights? We hope not, because a quick pull on the balloon-release cord and "bon voyage, the canine is airborne!"

Pick a nice spot on the ground to watch the "Fido Flight." As he drifts off into the sunset and his yelps get fainter and fainter, you might wish to make use of the included high-powered binoculars we've thoughtfully provided to get one last glimpse of the little guy.

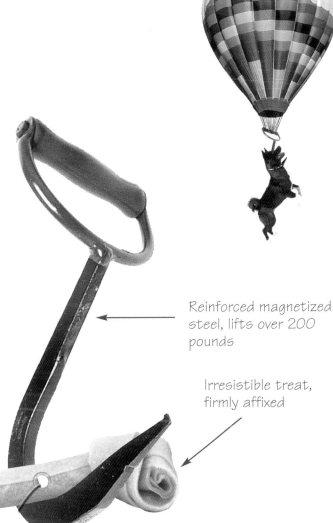

Reinforced magnetized steel, lifts over 200 pounds

Irresistible treat, firmly affixed

Soft-Landing Package

For our squeamish customers who can't stand the thought of even the most evil Fido plummeting to earth, we offer our Soft-Landing Package.

Includes autopilot, chase car* with mattress on roof, picnic lunch with Champagne, and a guaranteed soft landing (possibly).

Just follow Fido's flight carefully and position chase car underneath during descent (it works sometimes).

They'll be scared out of their fur on the way up but simply drive under them with this mattress and when they land they'll exclaim happily, *"Gee, that Buffy is such a great cat!"*

* Choice of Range Rover or Porsche Cayenne

Wow...I didn't think he'd go _that_ high!

Truck Delivery Only

Item #1243
Hot-Air Balloon Hook. Includes 60 ft. balloon, release cord, 4 helium tanks, binoculars..........$627.00
Soft-Landing Package. Incudes above items plus items listed at left..............................$64,887.00

Charter Boat Sailing Expedition
Take family and friends
No more minnows!

Shown: Muffy and Blarney, members of *The Ultimate Cats' Catalog* staff, testing the waters.

Forget the minnows, baby! You're going deep—where the water is green and deep, too.

We had so much positive feedback to last year's Lake Geneva, WI, Bass Day event we decided to go all the way. This incredible, all-inclusive package picks you up at your hotel and whisks you away to the deep blue sea. Your destination? The island of Martinique and its enchanting beaches and crystal-clear waters!

Your 56-foot sailing vessel is professionally crewed so all you have to do is enjoy the scenery and relax while taking in that invigorating salt air.

Of course, the fishing is great too, so here's your chance to see what tuna look like before they become fish heads.

You work hard, with all that mousing, dining, and napping. So reward yourself. You deserve it! Take your family or friends (the package is for 6).

Swimming lessons available.

Not convinced?

Ask for our free video of last year's event. See how Sniffles of Mt. Prospect, IL, caught her first bass and how Butch fought a life-and-death duel with a 12 pounder and landed the fish of his dreams. You'll see—our fishing expedition packages are great!

Call for price.

ORDER FORM
Indulge yourself. You're a cat . . . you deserve it!

How to order using your human's credit card
It's fun—it's easy—it's illegal! (But they never press charges)

Hi—I'm Snuggles. I'll be on the phone to help you. Just follow the easy steps below.

(1) Select the item(s) you want

(2) Have credit card ready*

(3) Dial (555) HAHAHUMAN

(4) At the tone, meow as follows:

    1 for MasterCharge

    2 for Visa

    3 for American Express

    4 for Discover

    5 for Target

(5) At the prompt, enter card number and expiration date by pressing the proper buttons with your paw.

(6) When you hear the tone indicating your(?) card is valid, enter item numbers. Don't worry, we'll total everything properly after we add shipping, handling, and tax. Sometimes we add some extra, but what do you care!

(7) Place card carefully back where you found it (wipe off paw prints!).

* If your card is platinum in color, go back to step (1) and select more items.

Item #	Description	Quantity	Color/Size	Price

NO NEED TO FILL IN THIS FORM. SEE ABOVE TO PHONE IN YOUR ORDER.

Total — We'll take care of this. Trust us.

SHIP TO:

_____

Your Name   Your Human's Name

_____

Address

_____

City/State   Zip

Note: To avoid possible intercept of shipment by your human, shipping labels are clearly marked *"No adult signature required. Please leave behind bush by front door."*